BLACKS IN AMERICA
1954—1979

BLACKS IN AMERICA 1954-1979

BY FLORENCE JACKSON

Franklin Watts/*New York*/*London*/*Toronto*/*Sydney*/1980

Photographs courtesy of: United Press International: pp. 9, 17, 20, 24, 30, 35, 36, 43, 46, 61, 69; Wide World Photos: pp. 14, 29; U.S. Conference of Mayors: p. 49; Atlantic Records: p. 71.

Cover photograph courtesy of
United Press International

Library of Congress Cataloging in Publication Data

Jackson, Florence.
    Blacks in America, 1954–1979.

    Bibliography: p.
    Includes index.
    SUMMARY: Discusses the events of a 25-year period during which blacks emerged as a force in their attempts to gain political and cultural recognition and increased civil rights.
    1. Afro-Americans—Civil rights—Juvenile literature.   2. Afro-Americans—History—1877–1964—Juvenile literature.   3. Afro-Americans—History—1964—Juvenile literature. [1. Afro-Americans—Civil rights.   2. Afro-Americans—History—1877–1964. 3. Afro-Americans—History—1964–   ] I. Title.
E185.61.J135   973'.0496073   80–15180
ISBN 0–531–02176–9

CONTENTS

WITH ALL
DELIBERATE SPEED

"The people of the South will never accept this monstrous decision," declared Mississippi Senator James Eastland after learning of the United States Supreme Court decision which stated that segregated schools were legally wrong. However, southerners did not all react the same way. Some were calm and readily accepted the decision. Others decided to wait and see what might happen. Still others, especially whites in the Deep South, were angry and bitter about the decision. This last group felt that their segregated way of life was threatened.

In contrast, black people rejoiced as the first part of a long struggle was over. For two years, the *Brown* v. *Board of Education of Topeka* case was listened to in court after court. Now, in 1954, the highest court in the nation ruled against a practice that was found in both the North and the South. Furthermore, the National Association for the Advancement of Colored People (NAACP), whose legal department led the fight, had won a major legal battle in education.

The Supreme Court judges understood that time would be needed to desegregate the public schools because of different local school problems. However, little effort was made toward desegregating the schools, so on May 31, 1955, the Court ordered public school authorities to obey the 1954 ruling "with all deliberate speed." Chief Justice Earl Warren gave the opinion of the Court:

> *While giving weight to these public and private considerations, the courts will require that the defendants make a prompt and reasonable start toward full compliance with our May 17, 1954 ruling.*

The NAACP moved quickly to support the May 31 ruling of the Supreme Court. On June 4, NAACP officials called an emergency meeting to map a program of action to implement the 1954 and 1955 decisions. Representatives from sixteen southern states and the District of Columbia attended, and the following statement was agreed upon at the meeting:

> *We authorize our branches in every state to act to secure desegregation beginning next September, by filing petitions with their school boards requesting the "prompt" beginning set forth in the May 31 opinion.*

In fact, the following suggested eight-step plan of action was sent to all NAACP branch offices to indicate how the statement was to be implemented:

1. File at once a petition with each school board, calling attention to the May 31 decision . . . .

2. Follow up the petition with periodic inquiries of the board seeking to determine what steps it is making to comply with the Supreme Court decision.

3. All during June, July, August and September, and thereafter, through meetings, forums, debates, conferences, etc., use every opportunity to explain what the May 31 decision means. . . .

4. Organize the parents in the community so that as many as possible will be familiar with the procedure when and if law suits are begun in behalf of plaintiffs and parents.

5. Seek the support of individuals and community groups, particularly in the white community, through churches, labor organizations, civic organizations and personal contact.

6. When announcement is made of the plans adopted by your school board, get the exact text of the school board's pronouncements and notify the State Conference and the National Office at once so that you will have the benefit of their views as to whether the plan is one which will provide for effective desegregation. . . .

7. If no plans are announced or no steps towards desegregation taken by the time school begins this fall, 1955, the time for a law suit has arrived. At this stage court action is essential. . . .

8. At this stage the matter will be turned over to the (NAACP) Legal Department and it will proceed with the matter in court. . . .

Southern opposition and resistance to the desegregation laws developed quickly. In less than two months after the 1954 decision, a White Citizens Council aimed at fostering segregation was formed in Mississippi. Other councils, usually made up of business and professional people, were organized in several southern states. The Ku Klux Klan, which was established after the Civil War, continued to draw members from working-class people.

These groups used various means to resist the desegregation of public schools. Sometimes black parents who tried to enroll their children in white schools lost their jobs or found that credit and loans became difficult to obtain. Whites who were in favor of desegregated schools also found that they received similar treatment.

One group which opposed desegregation received nationwide attention. Nineteen Senators and eighty-one members of the House of Representatives from eleven southern states signed and presented a statement against the school desegregation decisions made by the United States Supreme Court. Largely the work of Senator Sam J. Ervin of North Carolina, the statement praised those states which intended to resist desegregation through lawful means. The statement became known as the Southern Manifesto. It was considered significant that there were no signatures from the states of Delaware, Kentucky, Maryland, Missouri, Oklahoma, and West Virginia even though segregated school systems existed within those states.

The signers of the Southern Manifesto presented the argument that the Constitution did not mention education and that the Supreme Court abused its judicial power in the school cases. They also stated that the Court's action was done without the consent of the people and was "certain to destroy the system of public education in some of the States." Moreover, those states which declared that they would resist the integration of their schools were commended. Finally, the signers stated:

> *We pledge ourselves to use all lawful means to bring about a reversal of this decision which is contrary to the Constitution and to prevent the use of force in its implementation.*

Ten states and the District of Columbia obeyed the law. Alabama, Mississippi, and South Carolina did nothing to help desegregation. A series of court cases to oppose desegregation came from Florida, Georgia, Louisiana, and Virginia. In 1957, violence occurred in Arkansas, and in September, 1959, schools in Prince Edward County, Virginia, closed down and did not reopen until the Supreme Court ordered a decree to guarantee public education for black children in the county on May 25, 1964. On June 3, the Prince Edward County Board of Supervisors voted 4 to 2 to reopen public schools.

Nine black students were scheduled to be admitted to Central High School in Little Rock, Arkansas, on September 3 as part of a larger school board desegregation plan. However, Arkansas Governor Orval Faubus sent National Guard units to the school on September 2 to keep the plan from being used. Under Governor Faubus's order, the National Guard blocked the school entrance to the black students.

Governor Faubus's action and the mob violence which developed received national attention. And soon attention was on Washington, D.C. What was to be done about the rioting and violence in Little Rock, Arkansas, to keep nine black students from attending Central High School? President Eisenhower responded by sending Federal troops to Little Rock to see that Central High School admitted black students. It was not until September 23 that the students were admitted.

It was ten years after the Brown decision before any significant desegregation could be seen. In 1964, the passage of the Civil Rights Act gave the federal government an opportunity to withhold funds from segregated school districts. This in turn helped to enforce the 1954 law. Several court decisions stopped the delaying tactics and began efforts to desegregate northern schools.

Fifteen years later, the United States Supreme Court found it necessary to make another decision about school segregation. In October 1969, the Court issued a new order: " 'All deliberate speed' for desegregation is no longer constitutionally permissible. . . . The obligation of every school district is to terminate dual school systems at once." The decision was the opinion of all the justices.

Twenty years after the Brown decision, it was found that southern schools were far more integrated than northern schools. In fact, a 1972 survey by the Department of Health, Education and Welfare revealed that 46 percent of black students in southern states attend schools with a white majority, compared with only 28 percent in the North and West.

To increase the desegregation in the South, the United States Supreme Court on April 20, 1971, upheld by a vote of 9 to 0 the use of busing as a means to "dismantle the dual school systems of the South." But the Court made it clear that the decision did not apply to northern segregation based on neighborhood schools. In many northern urban areas students are assigned to their neighborhood schools which are segregated mainly because of segregated housing. The Court held that busing was proper unless "the time or distance is so great as to risk either the health of the children or significantly impinge on the educational process."

Many southerners were against busing. However, what came to be known as the great school busing controversy started in the northern city of Pontiac, Michigan. In August 1971, the Ku Klux Klan bombed ten school buses there, and from that time on busing was a national issue. The busing issue was debated for several years and erupted into violence in the city of Boston in 1975. Strong feeling for and against busing still remains. In 1976 a crowd of demonstrators who were against busing marched to the Capitol to urge Congress to block court-ordered busing. The demonstrators were a mixture of labor people, Ku Klux Klan members, Wallace-for president supporters, and long-time anti-busing people from Detroit and Boston.

Today, Central High School in Little Rock, Arkansas, which in 1957 needed federal troops to enforce integration, is considered a model of peaceful integration. Its enrollment is divided evenly between blacks and whites. Racial violence has practically disappeared. Student organizations such as athletic teams, cheerleading squads, student government, and elective offices are divided about evenly between blacks and whites.

In an examination of the results of the *Brown* decision, some individuals feel that even though integration seems rather slow in many parts of the nation, if, as noted black writer Robert Maynard of *The Washington Post* says, ". . . they look at schools alone, they will have missed the point of what Brown did." Maynard refers to the number of blacks now elected to political office and to the many cases involving discrimination in housing, employment, and recreation before the courts—all of them referring to the "equal protection of the law" clause of the Fourteenth Amendment used in the *Brown* case. The same clause is now used by groups in movements for such causes as equal rights for women. Maynard says, "Brown is a symbol of the start of the era of liberation movements in this country."

BOYCOTT: THE BEGINNING OF A MOVEMENT

In Montgomery, Alabama, on December 1, 1955, Mrs. Rosa Parks, a black woman, found a seat on the Cleveland Avenue bus. In those days, the buses had front seats reserved for whites only and seats in the rear for blacks. When all the seats for whites became filled, the bus driver would often ask black persons to give their seats to the whites. On this particular day, when the white section was filled, the bus driver asked Mrs. Parks to give her seat to a white man who had boarded the bus. She refused to get up. The driver threatened to call the police. But still Mrs. Parks did not move. Finally, the driver summoned the police and Mrs. Parks was arrested.

Black leaders in Montgomery became angry. They, along with black people in general, did not like how their people were treated on the city buses. And now, a black woman was arrested for refusing to give her seat to a white man. Furthermore, many people felt that the reason for this arrest was not lawful under the United States Constitution, which provides for "equal protection of the laws." Black and white people were not being treated equally.

What could be done about Mrs. Parks' arrest? More than forty black leaders and ministers representing almost every black organization met to discuss the situation on the following evening. One of the ministers at the meeting was Dr. Martin Luther King, Jr.

A proposal calling for a boycott of the city buses by blacks was presented. The leaders and ministers agreed that a boycott should take place. The idea would be presented to the black

Rosa Parks was accompanied by her lawyer (right) and a deputy on her way to jail after having been arrested for violating Montgomery, Alabama's, segregation laws on December 1, 1955.

community in the churches on Sunday morning. The people also would be asked to attend a mass meeting on Monday evening.

On Sunday morning, black ministers throughout Montgomery reported the Rosa Parks arrest to their congregations. They also emphasized their approval of a one-day boycott. Leaflets asking black people not to ride the city buses on Monday, December 5, were printed and distributed around the city to black churches, organizations, and businesses. Others were placed in the mailboxes of black people.

The leaders decided that an organization was needed to plan and direct the boycott. Dr. Martin Luther King, Jr., was elected by all present to be president of the organization. Ralph Abernathy, another minister, suggested the name *Montgomery Improvement Association* (MIA).

On Monday, old black people and young black people walked to work, school, and wherever else they wanted to go. In his book *Stride Toward Freedom* Dr. King described the scene that day:

> *Fortunately, a bus stop was just five feet from our house. . . . I was in the kitchen drinking my coffee when I heard Coretta cry, "Martin, Martin, come quickly!" I put down my cup and ran toward the living room. As I approached the front window Coretta pointed joyfully to a slowly moving bus: "Darling, it's empty!" I could hardly believe what I saw. I knew that the South Jackson line, which ran past our house, carried more Negro passengers than any other line in Montgomery, and that this first bus was usually filled with domestic workers going to their jobs. . . . Eagerly we waited for the next bus. . . . like the first, it was empty. A third bus appeared, and it too was empty of all but two white passengers. . . . All day long it con-*

tinued. At the afternoon peak the buses were still as empty of Negro passengers as they had been in the morning. Students of Alabama State College, who usually kept the South Jackson bus crowded, were cheerfully walking or thumbing rides. Job holders had either found other means of transportation or made their way on foot. While some rode in cabs or private cars, others used less conventional means. Men were seen riding mules to work, and more than one horse-drawn buggy drove the streets of Montgomery that day.

During the rush hours the sidewalks were crowded with laborers and domestic workers, many of them well past middle age, trudging patiently to their jobs and home again, sometimes as much as twelve miles.

Black people dramatized their total support for Rosa Parks by boycotting the city buses. But later that day, Mrs. Parks was found guilty of refusing to give up her seat and was fined ten dollars, plus four dollars for court costs. Mrs. Parks' conviction was very important. Dr. King wrote, "It was a test for the validity of the segregation law itself."

Monday night more than three thousand people met at the Holt Street Baptist Church. Hundreds who could not get into the church listened to the proceedings on loudspeakers outside the building. Dr. King was the principal speaker. He gave the people a report on the Rosa Parks situation, and then he provided them with a sense of direction and a burning desire for justice. A resolution to continue the boycott until conditions changed was read at the meeting and accepted by all.

A call for volunteers with cars went out to the black community. About three hundred automobiles, private cars, and taxis were made available to pick up black people at different places around the city. The strategy proved successful. The buses remained empty. The Montgomery Improvement Association's leaders decided that it was time to demand that the city buses be desegregated. The city officials refused. In fact, some city commissioners announced that they would join the White Citizens Council.

Many meetings were held within the MIA and between the MIA and the city officials to work out an agreement about the treatment of black people on city buses. Dr. King, as president of MIA, was totally involved with all aspects of the protest and represented the organization at many different meetings.

On January 30, 1956, Dr. King attended an evening mass meeting at the First Baptist Church. While he was at the church, a bomb that was thrown at his home exploded on the porch. When Dr. King arrived at his home, he found an angry crowd and the police in front of the house. After checking to see if his wife and baby were safe, Dr. King went out to quiet the crowd. His major message was, "We must meet violence with nonviolence." He asked the crowd not to look for weapons or use any they might have to avenge the bombing. He also reminded the crowd that, "If I am stopped, this movement will not stop because God is with the movement." With this assurance, Dr. King dismissed the angry crowd. In response, the crowd assured Dr. King that they supported his leadership.

The boycott continued and the city officials reestablished a "get tough" policy. Mass arrests of black people took place. Some persons were arrested for minor or nonexistent traffic violations. Others, waiting at pick-up points in white neighborhoods, were arrested for vagrancy. Drivers of the car pools were stopped and questioned about their licenses, car insurance, and places of work.

After the boycott was pronounced illegal by a Montgomery County grand jury, more than one hundred persons were indicted. Dr. King was among those indicted and later one of the eighty-nine convicted.

The "get tough" policy failed and the boycott continued. Finally, the city officials decided to take legal action to stop the car pool by suing the MIA, several churches, and some individuals. During the hearing on November 13, 1956, startling news arrived from Washington, D.C. Dr. King was handed the following news release:

> *The United States Supreme Court today affirmed a decision of a special three-judge U.S. District Court in declaring Alabama's state and local laws requiring segregation on buses unconstitutional. The Supreme Court acted without listening to any argument; it simply said "the motion to affirm is granted and the Judgment is affirmed."*

That night, as a last attempt to frighten black people, the Ku Klux Klan rode in their white robes and hoods through the black community.

On December 21, over twelve months after the boycott began, Dr. King and other leaders of the MIA sat in the front of a bus and rode through the streets of Montgomery. Glenn Smiley, a white minister and a native southerner, sat next to Dr. King during the triumphant ride. Dr. King wrote:

> *there comes a time when people get tired of being trampled by oppression. There comes a time when people get tired of being plunged into the abyss of exploitation and nagging injustice. The story of Montgomery is the story of 50,000 such Negroes who were*

After having been found guilty and fined $500 for conspiracy in leading the Montgomery bus boycott, Dr. Martin Luther King, Jr. vowed at a crowded church meeting to continue the boycott of city busses.

willing to substitute tired feet for tired souls, and walk
the streets of Montgomery until the walls of segrega-
tion were finally battered by the forces of justice.

Most whites accepted the integrated buses, but a few refused. A few blacks were assaulted when following the new system, shots were fired at integrated buses, and churches and homes were bombed. Ralph Abernathy, King's assistant in the MIA, had both his home and his church bombed in one night. Five whites were indicted for the bombings, but in spite of their signed confessions, there were no convictions.

However, the success of the MIA inspired blacks in other southern cities. It became apparent that an organization which could coordinate activities related to transportation and integration was needed. On January 10, 1957, the Southern Christian Leadership Conference on Transportation and Nonviolent Integration was established by Dr. King and clergymen from other southern cities. Sometime later the organization became known as the Southern Christian Leadership Conference (SCLC), with Dr. King as president.

NEW FREEDOM
FIGHTERS

From 1957 to 1968, black people made great strides in obtaining both equal rights and equal opportunities. Young black people became a major force in the movement to demand equality. Their motto, "put your bodies on the line," was a way of saying that they were not afraid to do what was necessary to achieve equal rights. Large numbers of young black people found that one way to work for equality was to join newly established organizations such as the Southern Christian Leadership Conference, the Student Nonviolent Coordinating Committee (SNCC or SNICK) and the Congress of Racial Equality (CORE). The National Association for the Advancement of Colored People was for the most part left to legal tasks and lobbying.

Inspired by the United States Supreme Court's actions in the desegregation of both schools and Alabama's state and city buses, a few students at North Carolina Agricultural and Technical College in Greensboro felt that it was time for eating places in their city to be desegregated.

On February 1, 1960, four students from North Carolina Agricultural and Technical College went into the Greensboro Woolworth's store and sat at the lunch counter. No blacks were supposed to be served at the counter. No one asked the students for their orders. But the students did not move. They sat at the counter for an hour without ordering or eating. Because the students would not move, the lunch counter was closed earlier than usual for the day. This practice of sitting in places that were for whites only became known as a *sit-in*.

Julian Bond, then a student at Morehouse College in Atlanta, Georgia, reacted to the Greensboro sit-in by organizing a

On Feb. 1, 1960, four young black men sat down at a Woolworth's lunch counter in Greensboro, N.C., and triggered a movement that soon spread across the nation. In Feb. of 1980, Woolworth's invited the four men back for breakfast to celebrate the twentieth anniversary of the movement.

meeting of students at the college to discuss what had occurred. An outgrowth of that meeting was a sit-in demonstration in Atlanta, which turned out to be the best organized and largest of them all.

The use of sit-in demonstrations spread rapidly. Within two weeks after the first one in Greensboro, lunch-counter sit-ins were held in fifteen cities in five southern states. A new form of protest was established and its effect was widely felt.

To make the sit-ins even more effective, it was necessary to organize future demonstrations. A group of students who had sit-in experience was called together in Atlanta by Ella Baker of the SCLC office for a meeting in late February. SCLC gave $800 to the students to plan and organize sit-ins. With the money, the Student Nonviolent Coordinating Committee was established. In the fall of 1961, sixteen young college students left school to become the first group of dedicated SNCC fighters. By 1964, the number had increased to 1,500.

SNCC workers were both black and white students who came from either black colleges in the South or white colleges and universities in the North and the West. Most of the SNCC workers, however, were southern blacks.

Mississippi and Georgia, two states in the Deep South, became major targets for SNCC. Other states, such as Alabama, Virginia, Maryland, and Arkansas also received attention. SNCC workers believed in "direct action" and developed a program which took them into black communities. They encouraged blacks to register to vote, lead demonstrations, hold classes, and distribute food and clothing where necessary. SNCC workers believed in civil disobedience. They felt that nonviolent revolutionary tactics were necessary to move the white power structure which upheld segregation and inequality.

Soon newspapers around the country carried stories about SNCC leaders, demonstrations, and programs. Names such as Marion Barry, Julian Bond, Chuck McDew, John Lewis, James Forman, and Charles Sherrod were often in the news.

Whites resisted SNCC's activities to bring about equality. Some turned to violence. Blacks were beaten with clubs and chains and sometimes even shot. Some of their homes were bombed; others were thrown off their land. During demonstrations, police moved in with dogs, water hoses, and tear gas bombs to disperse the blacks. When the demonstrators refused to move, they were arrested and jailed. Violence occurred in Florida, Georgia, Kentucky, South Carolina, and Texas, as well as Mississippi, where the violence among both police and other whites was considered the worst of all the states.

CORE, which for a long time had used nonviolent direct action, took an active part in helping the youthful SNCC workers conduct classes in nonviolent techniques. Many of these classes, which took place at black colleges, were attended by hundreds of students. The students were trained to accept physical violence without fighting back. They were taught how to protect their heads, faces, and other vital parts of their bodies.

By April 1960, sit-ins had been planned and organized in sixty different centers. Ella Baker of SCLC, who had helped to establish SNCC, felt that the centers should be coordinated. She organized another meeting of young people who were interested or involved in sit-ins to discuss ways to communicate and to organize their activities. Over two hundred persons attended the meeting at Shaw University in Raleigh, North Carolina. Nineteen northern colleges and fifty-eight different southern communities sent delegates to the meeting.

After a second meeting in May, 1960, SNCC began to func-

Lunch counter sit-ins by blacks and white sympathizers became more numerous in the early sixties. Here, three demonstrators are shown at a Jackson, Mississippi, lunch counter covered with mustard, catsup, and sugar sprayed on them by angry white youths.

tion as a better coordinated organization. Marion Barry was elected chairman, and a publication entitled *The Student Voice* was published.

Some administrators of black colleges, however, became alarmed at the increasing number of their students involved in the sit-ins. Some of them feared that the white college trustees, state legislatures, and other involved officials who supported the colleges might cut off their funds. To avoid such harsh action from the white powers, some school administrators threatened to expel students and fire teachers who participated in the demonstrations. Many students, however, ignored the threats, and the sit-in movement expanded and used different tactics to call attention to injustices.

In February, 1961, ten students were arrested in Rock Hill, South Carolina. They refused bail and remained in jail. SNCC officials reacted by sending four of their members to Rock Hill to sit in and get themselves arrested also. By refusing bail and remaining in jail, the students could focus the attention of the nation and possibly the world on the injustice of segregation. This new type of protest became known as the "jail-no-bail" policy.

Still another type of protest emerged. But this time it was organized by CORE. On May 4, 1961, a group of seven blacks, including James Farmer, the new director of CORE, and six whites began a trip from Washington, D.C., to New Orleans, Louisiana. The group divided themselves between two buses, one a Greyhound and the other a Trailways. The group's purpose was to challenge segregated interstate buses and waiting rooms, which still existed even though the United States Supreme Court had ruled, in 1956, that segregation, on public buses was not legal. Members of the two groups were called *Freedom Riders*.

The two buses with their special passengers traveled through Virginia and North Carolina with few problems. However, in Rock Hill, South Carolina, John Lewis of SNCC and his white companion, Albert Bigelow, were attacked when they walked toward the Greyhound terminal's white waiting room. But these attacks did not stop the group. They continued on through Georgia and into Alabama. Near Anniston, Alabama, the Greyhound bus was stopped by a white mob. The tires were slashed and the entire bus was then burned. About an hour later, the Trailways bus arrived. A few whites boarded this second bus and began beating the blacks sitting in the front seats. Two of the white Freedom Riders tried to stop the white attackers, but they, too, were turned on and beaten. Then all the Freedom Riders were forced to ride at the back of the bus. At the next stop, Birmingham, Alabama, the Freedom Riders were beaten again by white hoodlums.

After the Birmingham attack, the Greyhound bus driver refused to take the group on to Montgomery. Finally, the Freedom Riders decided to fly to New Orleans so that they could join the anniversary celebration of the May 17, 1954, Supreme Court decision on school desegregation. A bomb threat cancelled their flight. But after a six-hour wait, the group flew on to New Orleans.

News about the Freedom Ride had been in the newspapers for almost two weeks which encouraged several other groups to send riders into Alabama. Although the first Freedom Ride was over, several members of CORE had remained in Montgomery. James Farmer joined the group and a second Freedom Ride began. Three other groups, the Nashville Student Movement, the Student Nonviolent Coordinating Committee, and the Southern Christian Leadership Conference, joined the CORE Freedom Riders. Several concerned people, including rabbis, white college professors, and other blacks and whites, also joined the Freedom Ride.

The United States attorney general, Robert Kennedy, had previously asked Alabama Governor John Patterson to provide state protection for the Freedom Riders. The governor agreed at first, then changed his mind. Both President John Kennedy and his brother the attorney general became quite concerned about the safety of the Riders and tried to reach Governor Patterson without success. The President, however, did reach the lieutenant governor. The next day, May 20, Governor Patterson said, "We are going to do all we can to enforce the laws of the state on the highways and everywhere else, but we are not going to escort these agitators. We stand firm on that position." That same day the FBI alerted the Montgomery police that a bus would be arriving in the city with some Freedom Riders and there would probably be some violence. As predicted, when the bus arrived there was violence. About six riders were beaten and the United States attorney general's representative, John Seigenthaler, was knocked unconscious. The police did not arrive until about ten minutes after the fighting began.

The attorney general ordered federal marshals to go to Montgomery to obtain an injunction against the Ku Klux Klan, the National States Rights Party, and other individuals who were interfering with the Freedom Riders. In addition, President Kennedy appealed again to Alabama state and city officials for order.

On May 21, more race rioting occurred, and the deputy attorney general arrived in Montgomery to direct the federal activities. Students began arriving from Tennessee, Louisiana, and New York to support the Freedom Riders. Another group of riders, this time on a "hate bus" organized by the American Nazi Party, left Washington, D.C., for New Orleans. The situa-

tion became even more tense. Martial law was proclaimed in Montgomery.

Many different demands were made by various individuals and groups. The attorney general called for action by the governor and local police. The Rotary Club of Montgomery demanded that the federal marshals be withdrawn. The Chamber of Commerce called for law and order. And the Junior Chamber of Commerce condemned the Freedom Riders and claimed disappointment with the failure of the city police to keep order. But the Freedom Riders announced that they would continue on to Jackson, Mississippi.

On their arrival in Jackson, Mississippi, the Freedom Riders were arrested. In New Orleans the "hate bus" riders were arrested for "unreasonably alarming the public." The attorney general asked for a cooling-off period but Dr. King, who by now had become active in these new protests, said no.

It was not until September 22 that the Interstate Commerce Commission issued an order banning segregation in interstate terminal facilities. The order, however, did not take effect until November 1.

An outcome of the Freedom Rides was that CORE proved the necessity of direct mass action to achieve the equal rights which the courts had granted.

Five "freedom riders" were arrested at a train station in 1961 for bringing a racially mixed group into a white waiting room.

TOWARD GREATER CIVIL RIGHTS

The success of the Montgomery bus boycott gave Dr. Martin Luther King, Jr., instant publicity throughout the nation. Inspired by success, Dr. King continued his work as a leader of black people by supporting their wishes for integration and joining them when it came time to protest.

As President of SCLC, Dr. King was able to inspire large numbers and to lead them in developing a civil rights program. SCLC members stressed four areas in their work. First, they worked with other civil rights groups in voter registration drives in Alabama, Georgia, and Mississippi. Second, they provided food, housing, and money to the Freedom Riders as they met with problems in various places along their route. Third, a major effort was made to assist the Student Nonviolent Coordinating Committee. Fourth, they provided a program, of citizenship training which helped community leaders gain knowledge of how to teach reading and writing, civics, voter registration techniques, and ways to evaluate political candidates.

Dr. King was a fitting leader of SCLC. In his youth he had experienced much of the discrimination that SCLC was fighting against. King was born in Atlanta, Georgia, on January 15, 1929. He attended public schools in Atlanta, then went on to Morehouse College. Soon after graduation, King attended Crozer Theological Seminary, where he studied for the ministry. He did further study at the University of Pennsylvania, Howard University, and finally Boston University, where he received a doctoral degree.

After graduation, King was offered several jobs. He took

the job of minister at the Dexter Avenue Baptist Church in Montgomery, Alabama, in 1954. The previous year Dr. King had married Coretta Scott, a music student whom he had met while studying in Boston.

Dr. King had been at the Dexter Avenue Baptist Church less than two years when he became involved in leading the Montgomery bus boycott. As president of SCLC, King participated in many demonstrations and stressed his belief in nonviolence. However, the demonstrations were met with violence from both citizens and police.

The largest number of mass demonstrations occurred from 1960 to 1963. Some demonstrations were led by the Reverend Fred Shuttlesworth, who had organized the Alabama Christian Movement for Human Rights (ACHR) in 1956. During the early sixties, the ACHR supported efforts to integrate the city's public places other than the bus or train stations and the airport. The protestors were resisted by city officials at every turn. One such official was Commissioner of Public Safety Eugene "Bull" Connor, who became known for his contempt for the rights of blacks and his disregard for the laws passed by the federal government. He was feared by both whites and blacks. Additional support for Connor's attitude was given by Governor George Wallace, who had pledged "segregation forever" in Alabama.

In April, 1963, King and his associates for the first time used civil disobedience, a disregard of a court order, when faced with a city-obtained court injunction. After several days of lunch-counter sit-ins, Birmingham city officials obtained an injunction to stop the sit-ins. However, Dr. King decided that in support of about five hundred persons already arrested and approximately three hundred who were still in jail, he, too, would get himself arrested by ignoring the new injunction. A group of about fifty people, including Ralph Abernathy and Dr. King, were arrested as they marched to the downtown area of Birmingham.

King was placed in solitary confinement. He could not receive any visitors, not even his lawyer. Dr. King's wife, Coretta, became concerned and decided to call President John Kennedy in Washington, D.C. Attorney General Robert Kennedy returned the call and told her that he would do everything he could to ease her husband's situation. A few hours later President Kennedy called Mrs. King from Palm Beach, Florida, to assure her that he, too, would work on the situation immediately. President Kennedy and the attorney general undoubtedly called the Birmingham officials, because as Dr. King wrote, "immediately after Coretta heard from them, my jailers asked if I wanted to call her. After the President's involvement, conditions changed considerably."

Many other demonstrations met with resistance. In Danville, Virginia, forty-seven of the sixty-five demonstrators were injured. High-powered fire hoses were used to direct streams of water at the protesters. In Birmingham, billy clubs were used by police on blacks. Electric cattle prods were used in Gadsden, Alabama. Churches that held mass meetings were burned to the ground. Homes were shot into or burned to the ground also.

On June 12, 1963, Medgar Evers, the Mississippi State NAACP field secretary, was killed outside his home in Jackson, Mississippi. In Birmingham, Alabama, four young black girls were killed during Sunday school classes when a bomb was thrown through the windows of the 16th Street Baptist Church.

In all, there were 930 protest demonstrations in 115 cities in eleven southern states during 1963. Finally, President Kennedy spoke to the nation:

Dr. Martin Luther King, Jr.
addressing a crowd of thousands during
the 1963 March on Washington.

One hundred years of delay have passed since President Lincoln freed the slaves, yet their heirs, their grandsons are not fully free. They are not yet freed from the bonds of injustice; they are not freed from social and economic oppression. And this nation, for all its boasts will not be fully free until all its citizens are free.

In response to the injustices which black people faced, A. Philip Randolph suggested a mass demonstration in Washington, D.C. What became known as the March on Washington was held on August 28, 1963. Blacks and whites, about 250,000 strong, marched on Washington, D.C., to urge Congress to pass a civil rights bill. In addition, the marchers called for equality in education, jobs, better housing, and public accommodations. They demanded the opportunity to vote and "freedom now" for all blacks. Dr. King delivered a stirring speech in which he told of his dream of freedom for all people.

While Dr. King was leading black people in the civil rights revolution, a religious group called the Black Muslims called for black people to separate themselves from whites. The Black Muslim movement began during the early 1930s in Detroit, Michigan. Many of the followers were recent migrants from the South who felt keenly about their oppression in their former homes and the limited freedom in the North.

One of the most influential men in the Black Muslim sect was Malcolm X. He became a major influence to many groups

Malcolm X spoke to reporters when he arrived in Washington in 1963 to set up headquarters for the Black Muslims in the nation's capital.

within the black community as he preached unity in order to achieve the liberation of black people.

Born Malcolm Little in Omaha, Nebraska, he grew up in Lansing, Michigan. As a child, he was influenced by his family's treatment by hostile whites, the unsympathetic feelings of social workers who worked with his family, and finally the breakup of his family. At the age of fifteen, he left school. Before he was twenty-one, Malcolm was serving time in prison for burglary. While in prison, he became interested in Islam; he joined the Black Muslims after leaving prison in 1962. At the same time, he dropped his surname and became Malcolm X. He became a very vocal leader of the Black Muslims. In 1964, however, he broke away and established his own Muslim mosque. Later he founded the Organization of Afro-American Unity, a nonreligious group aimed at furthering the liberation of black Americans.

In 1964, Malcolm X traveled to Africa and also made a pilgrimage to Mecca. A renewed drive to encourage unity among black people throughout the world resulted from this trip. He began to see a need to move away from the black separatist attitude of the Black Muslims. However, before he had an opportunity to pursue this new way of thinking, he was assassinated at a meeting in Harlem in 1965.

The Black Muslims stressed group solidarity among blacks. The leader Elijah Muhammad, his followers believed, was commissioned by Allah himself to "wake the sleeping black nation" and to rid black people of white domination. Today Black Muslims are established in almost every major city with a sizable black population. During the mid-seventies, however, the Black Muslims began to change their belief in black separatism to integration. Membership in the Black Muslim religious organization was soon opened to whites.

INTENSIFYING
THE FIGHT

In the fall of 1966, two young men, Huey P. Newton and Bobby G. Seale, organized the Black Panther Party for Self-Defense in Oakland, California. Seale was made chairman and Newton minister of defense of the organization. Newton was born in Louisiana in 1942. About a year later his family moved to California, where young Newton attended high school and later college, as well as six months of law school. Seale was born in Dallas, Texas, in 1936. He, too, moved with his family to California. Upon graduation from Oakland High School, young Seale attended Merritt College, where he met Huey Newton. They worked together to start courses in black history and to call attention to the need for more black instructors. They also worked at the North Oakland Poverty Center. They became members of the Afro-American Association at Merritt College but left the organization within a year because the members seemed ineffective in ending oppression in the ghetto.

Both young men admired Malcolm X and another black writer named Frantz Fanon. They also studied the works of the Soviet writers Lenin and Marx, as well as the Chinese leader Mao Zedong and the Vietnamese Ho Chi Minh. However, it was Malcolm X's stress on self-defense and his emphasis on freedom that deeply impressed Newton and Seale. They believed that blacks had to fight their oppressors in order to achieve dignity as a people.

One of the first problems of the ghetto to which the Panthers directed public attention was police brutality. The Panthers carried guns and law books as they trailed police cars through the slums of Oakland. When black people were stopped, the Panthers made sure that their constitutional rights were not violated. Black people in Oakland were impressed by the Panthers' ability to cut down on the amount of injustice. Soon the Panthers were involved in other areas, such as protesting rent evictions, teaching classes in black history, and informing people on welfare of their rights. Their work attracted many blacks, and the party's membership grew.

In 1967 a gun control bill which was designed to control the Panthers' right to carry guns was introduced in the California legislature. On May 2, while the bill was being debated, thirty armed Panthers walked up the steps of the capitol building. At the top, Bobby Seale read a statement of the Panthers' principles before walking into the visitors' gallery of the chambers. The police and press arrived shortly at the capitol. The presence of the Panthers, police, and reporters created some excitement in the chambers. But no violence occurred. The Panthers' statement was read again as they left the building. However, when they started to leave the capitol, police arrested the group and charged them with disturbing the peace. Bobby Seale and several other Panthers served a six-month prison sentence. The Panthers' efforts were all in vain. The gun control bill passed. But within a few months, Black Panther branches were established in Tennessee, Georgia, New York, Detroit, and Los Angeles. Eldridge Cleaver, another rising freedom fighter, and his wife Kathleen joined the organization. Stokely Carmichael, James Forman, and a new freedom fighter, H. Rap Brown, were named to important posts in the party at the rally. Because of a difference of opinion about creating alliances with whites, a rift grew between the Panthers and SNCC. The Panthers believed that they could work with whites to end the oppression of blacks. On the other hand, SNCC members felt that blacks alone should work on their liberation.

**H. Rap Brown (left) and Stokely Carmichael
at a 1967 press conference in Atlanta during
which it was announced that Brown was
succeeding Carmichael as head of SNCC.**

Angela Davis speaks to a crowd outside the Los Angeles City Hall in 1969.

A general fear of Black Panthers among a growing number of blacks helped to develop an intensifying desire to curtail their activities in 1969. The American Civil Liberties Union (ACLU) reported that "the record of police actions across the nation against the Black Panther Party forms a *prima facie* [based on first impression] case for the conclusion that law enforcement officials are waging a drive against the black militant organization resulting in various civil liberties violations." The ACLU also released a list of forty-eight major confrontations between police and Panthers.

In 1970, after two Panthers were killed while sleeping by Chicago police, an editorial in *The New York Times* stated:

> *The story unfolded by the Chicago grand jury makes it appear that the law-enforcement agencies, more than the Panthers, were acting out a conspiracy. The police, following Federal tips, sprayed the Panthers' lodging with massive gunfire, even though no more than one shot was found to have been fired from the inside. . . .*
>
> *Against a background of doctored evidence and coached police witnesses, it is not surprising that the State's Attorney, who initially had played a leading role in building the public case against the Panthers, finally dropped all charges against them.*

Other freedom fighters, such as Angela Davis, emerged during the struggle for black liberation during the late sixties. In 1968, Ms. Davis joined the Black Panther party in Los Angeles and participated in the political education program. She was teaching at the University of California at Los Angeles but was fired because she belonged to the Communist party. Ms. Davis became interested in the case of three black men, George Jackson, John

Clutchette, and Fleeta Drumgo, who were accused of killing a guard at Soledad Prison. There seemed to be no evidence that the three men were the actual killers. But they were held responsible for a rebellion of blacks in the tension-filled segregated prison which ended in the death of the guard. Sympathy for the three men motivated the establishment of the Soledad Brothers Defense Committee, to which Ms. Davis devoted some of her time.

On August 7, 1970, Jonathan Jackson, a younger brother of one of the Soledad Brothers, stopped a Marin County courtroom proceeding by pulling a gun and demanding that everyone freeze. Young Jackson and three others in the courtroom led Judge Harold Haley, the district attorney, and several jurors out to a parked van. As he left the courtroom, Jonathan shouted, "Free the Soledad Brothers by 12:30." After they entered the van, a barrage of shots fired at the van killed or wounded all inside. Judge Haley and the district attorney, Gary Thomas, were dead.

Angela Davis was not at the courthouse at the time of the shooting. However she became one of the FBI's most wanted criminals. She was charged by the state of California with kidnapping and murder in an alleged plot to free George Jackson in the incident. Upon her capture in New York City, Ms. Davis was returned to California to stand trial. In the meantime, George Jackson was transferred to San Quentin jail, where he was later killed in a shoot-out. Angela Davis was acquitted in July, 1972.

By 1979, only two of the several organizations that worked to gain civil rights for black people remained active. The Southern Christian Leadership Conference headed by Ralph Abernathy still operates a program. The National Association for the

Advancement of Colored People continues under the leadership of Executive Director Benjamin Hooks. A new organization, People United to Save Humanity (PUSH), led by the Reverend Jessie Jackson, continues the fight for both economic and civil rights.

DEVELOPING
POLITICAL STRENGTH

There exists a new breed of black politician who are considered "soul brothers" but who at the same time can obtain white votes as well as black votes to put and keep them in office. As the number of blacks in political offices increased, they found it necessary to hold a political convention.

In March, 1972, the first National Black Political Convention was held in Gary, Indiana. Over 3,330 delegates who held elected public offices such as mayor, alderman, city councilman, or member of a state legislature, as well as district leaders, elected officials' aides, and community representatives attended the convention. Including official observers, there were more than eight thousand black Americans who had put aside their differences to meet and plan for meeting black political needs. The participants represented a variety of views and political affiliations: for example, Samuel C. Jackson, an assistant secretary of Housing and Urban Development in the Nixon administration; Bobby Seale, a founder of the Black Panther party; and the Reverend Jesse L. Jackson, director of People United to Save Humanity (PUSH) among others.

The black mayor of Gary, Richard G. Hatcher, was the keynote speaker. His speech reflected what he saw as a need to build black strength within the Democratic and Republican parties:

> *This convention signals the end of hip-pocket politics. We ain't in nobody's hip pocket no more. We say to the two political parties this is their last chance. They have had too many already. These are not idle threats. . . . I, for one, am willing to give the two major po-*

*litical parties one more chance in the year 1972. But
if they fail us, a not unlikely prospect, we must then
seriously probe the possibility of a third party movement in this country.*

The Reverend Jesse Jackson was more direct and called for the
creation of "a black political party."

A document entitled *The National Black Political Agenda*
was drawn up at the convention. It is an historically significant
document reflecting major concerns of black Americans in 1972.
The agenda is made up of two political action checklists. The
first list contains sixty-three items to be implemented by a committee of the National Black Political Convention. This checklist is called the "Action Agenda for Black People" and is divided into eight categories: political empowerment, economic
empowerment, human development, international policy and
black people, communications, rural development, environment
protection, and self-determination for the District of Columbia.

The second checklist is called the "Action Agenda for Political Office Holders and Seekers." The same eight categories
are used and 140 items are included.

The first item in the agenda is a call for the creation of a
National Black Assembly as an outgrowth of the National Black
Political Convention:

*We need [a] permanent political movement that ad-
dresses itself to the basic control and reshaping of
American institutions that currently exploit black
America and threaten the whole society.*

It ends with the statement:

*This is our challenge at Gary and beyond, for a new
black politics demands new vision, new hope and new*

definition of the possible. Our time has come. These things are necessary. All things are possible.

Black unity was threatened because issues involving independent black politics vied with the theory of building black strength within the Democratic and Republican parties. A call for Israel to give up Arab territory taken in the 1967 war and a resolution against forced busing to achieve racial balance in schools were also heatedly discussed at the convention. But the general reaction of the delegates was that they were happy to attend. Many of the participants felt that black Americans, who had set the style for social protests during the last two decades, might do the same for a new brand of politics.

By 1974, however, the black nationalists, who were generally against integration and believed that blacks alone should control their political, economic, and social affairs, caused some of the expected participants to stay away and others who did attend to think about ending their membership.

Some blacks in national politics had already gained recognition. Assemblywoman Yvonne Braithwaite Burke from California was elected cochairwoman of the 1972 Democratic Convention. Basil Paterson was already vice-chairman of the Democratic National Committee and would later become secretary of state in New York. And Congresswoman Shirley Chisholm of New York became the first black woman to seek a major-party Presidential nomination. In 1974 two blacks were elected to the office of lieutenant governor of their states. In California, State Senator Mervyn Dymally and in Colorado, State Legislator George L. Brown won their races for lieutenant governor. Congressman Charles B. Rangel of New York became the first black to be named to the powerful House Ways and Means Committee. Other blacks were named to seats on the House Rules and Appropriations Committee. By the mid-seven-

**Rep. Shirley Chisholm, a candidate for the
Democratic presidential nomination, shakes hands
with well-wishers in Raleigh, North Carolina.**

ties, blacks had a greater voice on important committees than at any other time in Congressional history.

There was one black man not in politics who has been written about as "the man who toppled a president." In June 1972, Frank Wills, a 26-year-old black security guard at the Watergate apartment houses discovered a break-in at the Democratic party headquarters and called the police. It was discovered that the break-in was masterminded by Republicans on the White House staff. Attempts to conceal President Nixon's knowledge of the break-in cover-up failed and in turn led to the beginning of a scandal that forced President Nixon to resign. Many top members of the President's White House staff involved in the scandal were jailed.

By 1975 the National Black Assembly was in deep trouble. The Assembly decided to run an independent black presidential candidate in 1976. Moreover, the position of Imamu Baraka (formerly known as LeRoi Jones), who dominated the Assembly, and others that integration had no connection with black needs caused dissatisfaction among many of the delegates.

Another group of politicians formed a Black Caucus made up of black members of the House of Representatives. In 1969 six black members of the House started meeting to discuss issues related to blacks. The group formally organized in 1971 and by 1976 grew to sixteen members and offered an unofficial motto which states, "We have no permanent friends, no permanent enemies, just permanent interests, the interests of our black and minority constituents."

When the Caucus was formed, its members were viewed as national heroes by many blacks, and great achievements were expected of them. They were seen as a new kind of black leadership by committee instead of leadership by well-known individuals such as Dr. Martin Luther King, Stokely Carmichael, or Roy Wilkins.

The Caucus gained national attention when its members boycotted President Nixon's 1971 State of the Union address on the ground that he had refused to meet with the Black Caucus, at which time he was to have been presented with more than sixty recommendations. In response to the black legislators' push for action, President Nixon appointed a group to study the recommendations. However, President Nixon later rejected most of the recommendations.

In May, 1976, another meeting was held to explore the question of black political power and find a way to have more of an impact on the political process. Several similar meetings were held after 1971 but over the years there were always problems which were seemingly unsolvable. For example, some blacks feel that the Democrats take the black vote for granted while the Republicans ignore it. Some black leaders believe that their political influence and their ability to help their supporters have not kept up with the increasing number of blacks in political office. Attempts to run a black for president or to form a black political party have ended in failure.

One of the most prominent Democrats in the country, Barbara Jordan, was a keynote speaker at the 1976 Democratic Convention; her mere presence on the speakers platform quieted the noisy convention hall. She said:

There is something different and special about this opening night. I am a keynote speaker.

In the interesting years since 1832, it would have been most unusual for any national political party to have asked a Barbara Jordan to make a keynote address—most unusual.

The past notwithstanding, a Barbara Jordan is before you tonight. This is one additional bit of evidence

Keynote speaker Rep. Barbara Jordan of Texas was the powerful final act in the opening day of the 1976 Democratic National Convention.

that the American dream need not forever be deferred. . . .

We must provide the people with a vision of the future that is attainable. . . . We must strike a balance between the idea that the government can do everything and the belief that the government should do nothing.

Barbara Jordan was born in Houston, Texas, in 1936. She attended the segregated public schools in Houston and the all-black Texas Southern University. She decided to attend law school after briefly thinking about becoming a chemist or a pharmacist. When asked why she chose law instead, Ms. Jordan answered, "Who ever heard of an outstanding pharmacist?" She learned early in her career that "it was necessary to be backed by money, power and influence." Furthermore, Ms. Jordan said, "To be effective, I had to get inside the club, not just inside the chamber."

Black people voted in record numbers in the 1976 election, helping to elect Jimmy Carter of Georgia the new president of the United States. There was hope among blacks that their support would result in the appointment of a black cabinet member. President Carter instead decided to name a young black by the name of Andrew J. Young as United States Ambassador to the United Nations. Ambassador Young later resigned from the position, however, after a controversy over his meeting with a member of the Palestine Liberation Army.

PROBLEMS
OF CITY LIFE

By the early seventies, there were black mayors in Cleveland, Ohio; Gary, Indiana; Chapel Hill, North Carolina; Fayette, Mississippi; Atlanta, Georgia; Detroit, Michigan; Newark, New Jersey; and a chief executive in the District of Columbia. Numerous small cities had black mayors also, for a total of about 98 blacks serving as mayors of American cities. Furthermore, it was significant that growing numbers of whites supported and helped many of these black mayors to win their elections.

Respect for the ability of one of the black mayors was demonstrated in 1974 when Kenneth Gibson of Newark, New Jersey, was elected the first black chairman of the advisory board of the United States Conference of Mayors. From that position, he had an opportunity to become the first black president of the organization which represents the mayors of the nation's cities.

However, almost all of the new black mayors who took over cities were faced with new and changing situations. Cities not long ago were the centers of life. The jobs and services were there; the major shopping areas were there. People generally looked to the cities for cultural and recreational activities. By the early seventies, however, businesses had moved to shopping centers outside the cities; hotels had closed and motels had opened along the highways; colleges had moved to campuses in rural areas; theaters and other kinds of recreational centers began to open in suburban areas.

The black population of the central cities is increasing. For many years, whites, especially those with school-age children have been moving out of the central cities, leaving behind a

*In 1976, Mayor Kenneth Gibson of
Newark was installed as the first black
president of the U.S. Conference
of Mayors by out-going president
Mayor Moon Landrieu of New Orleans.*

growing number of nonwhite people. In an examination of the figures, it has been found that in 1950, 43 percent of all blacks lived in central cities, compared with 34 percent of all whites. By 1966, 56 percent of all blacks were central city residents, compared to only 27 percent of all whites. Furthermore, it has been predicted that by 1985, 60 percent of all nonwhites will be central city residents. The growing black population of the cities as well as the efforts to increase political awareness and voter registration have provided greater opportunities for blacks to obtain high-level city government jobs. Numerous studies indicate that the changing cities have a high percentage of poor blacks.

Adding to the complications for city governments is the fact that many of the people who still live in the cities also include the disabled and the aged, who require additional special services.

Housing conditions in inner cities have declined. The downtown areas of many cities have developed into slums. Businesses have moved to shopping centers outside the cities, leaving many vacant stores. Residential areas have also turned into slums as the high costs of fuel and general maintenance of buildings have caused many landlords to abandon their buildings, often with the tenants still living in them. New housing is mainly for the upper middle class, leaving the poor to search for the housing rejected by those who have fled to the suburbs or who can afford the new high-rental apartments.

Crime in the cities has risen to new highs, a fact which has alarmed both the officials and the citizens. In fact, the high incidence of crime in poverty areas is documented by police statistics. Some of the crimes are committed in order to pay for drugs. It has been found that a majority of heroin addicts are poor people living in slum neighborhoods. And by the mid-seventies, the average drug addict needed about forty-five dollars a day to maintain the habit, in addition to what was needed for food, shelter, and any other necessities.

Other problems of the cities facing the newly elected black mayors include transportation, pollution, garbage collection, education, and taxes.

In 1967, ten southern black small town mayors and their staffs met with housing and community development specialists guided by the Federal Housing Assistance Council to help one another solve their problems. They identified the following problems.

1. There was usually no system to deliver needed social services when black mayors replaced white mayors, mostly because the previous administrations did not choose to seek help for the poor and often because they were suspicious of federal dollars, with their requirements of nondiscrimination and other obligations.

2. Since blacks were kept out of positions of responsibility previously, many were unfamiliar with the workings of the layer-upon-layer authorities such as the county, regional, state, and federal agencies and governments.

3. The outgoing white administrations lost political power but almost always kept the economic power in the community. They owned the land often needed for new housing as well as for job-producing expansion in industry and were often unwilling to part with it easily.

4. The new mayors in the small towns are often poor themselves and did not have the economic power to make improvements and are sometimes reluctant to ask for aid from agencies they suspected are racist.

The conditions in the central cities are believed to be among the major causes of the riots and mass demonstrations which occurred in the sixties and early seventies. The frequency and nationwide occurrence of disorders within cities caused much alarm. President Lyndon Baines Johnson addressed the nation on July 27, 1967, and said:

> *The only genuine, long range solution for what has happened lies in an attack—mounted at every level—upon the conditions that breed despair and violence. All of us know what those conditions are: ignorance, discrimination, slums, poverty, disease, not enough jobs. We should attack these conditions—not because we are frightened by conflict, but because we are fired by conscience. We should attack them because there is simply no other way to achieve a decent and orderly society in America.*

On July 28, the president established the National Advisory Commission On Civil Disorders and directed the members to answer three questions about the riots.

What happened?
Why did it happen?
What can be done to prevent it from happening again?

The commission came to a basic conclusion: "Our nation is moving toward two societies, one black, one white—separate and unequal." The commission identified the following places where disturbances occurred.

1963

Birmingham, Alabama
Savannah, Georgia

Cambridge, Maryland
Chicago, Illinois
Philadelphia, Pennsylvania

1964

Jacksonville, Florida
Cleveland, Ohio
St. Augustine, Florida
Philadelphia, Mississippi
Jersey City, New Jersey
Elizabeth, New Jersey
Paterson, New Jersey
Rochester, New York
New York City (Bedford-Stuyvesant and Harlem)
Chicago, Illinois
Philadelphia, Pennsylvania

1965

Selma, Alabama
Los Angeles, California
Elizabeth, New Jersey

1966

Los Angeles, California (Watts)
Chicago, Illinois
Cleveland, Ohio

1967

Tampa, Florida
Cincinnati, Ohio

Northern New Jersey
    Elizabeth, Plainfield,
    Englewood, Jersey City,
    New Brunswick, Newark
Atlanta, Georgia
Detroit, Michigan

The commission made many recommendations, of which the major ones were:

Employment

A comprehensive national manpower policy to meet the needs of both the unemployed and the underemployed. The policy will require:

- Continued emphasis on national economic growth and job creation.

- Unified and intensive recruiting to reach those who need help with information about available jobs, training, and supportive aids.

- Careful evaluation of the individual's vocational skills, potentials, and needs.

- Concentrated job-training efforts.

- Opening up existing public and private job structures to provide greater mobility for the underemployed.

- Large-scale development of new jobs in the public and private sectors to absorb as many as possible of the unemployed.

- Stimulation of public and private investment in depressed areas, both urban and rural.

- New kinds of assistance to those who will continue to be attracted to the urban centers.

- Increasing small business and other entrepreneurial opportunities in poverty areas, both urban and rural.

Education

- Increasing efforts to eliminate de facto segregation.

- Providing quality education for ghetto schools.

- Improving community-school relations.

- Expanding opportunities for higher and vocational opportunities.

Welfare

- Overhaul the present system (standards of assistance, extension of the Aid for Dependent Children program, work incentives and training, removal of freeze on recipients, and elimination of some restrictions on eligibility).

- Development of a national system of income supplementation to provide a basic floor of economic and social security for all Americans.

Housing

- Expansion on a massive basis of the supply of housing suitable for low-income families.

- Open up areas outside ghetto neighborhoods to occupancy by racial minorities.

General concern about the fate of both the cities and the people who live in them continues. During the summer of 1975, dozens of municipal, community, and police officials, as well as federal officials and social scientists, were interviewed in New York, New Haven, Providence, Philadelphia, Washington, D.C., Richmond, Chicago, and Los Angeles. As reported in *The New York Times,* there was little disagreement among the persons interviewed that the recession had hit blacks particularly hard and that as the economy improves, the impact will not be felt in pockets of poverty as quickly as elsewhere. "Further, some theorists are convinced that indelible scars will be left on the black community." One observer remarked that "there is a nervous restlessness in the ghetto. . . . It's like a volcano, . . . , peaceful and quiet. But you know it could erupt at any time, now or five years from now. It's scary." The peacefulness continued throughout the seventies. But, for how much longer?

PROTEST IN
THE THEATER

Frederick O'Neal, a black man, was president of Actors Equity Association, the leading organization for actors in the United States, from 1964 to 1973. O'Neal's position, however, was not an indication that blacks have achieved equality in American theater. Although blacks have a long history in black theater, only a limited number of their plays had been performed in the major white theater houses before the 1970s.

During the 1960s, the civil rights revolution opened some activities in American life to black people. Theater, the showcase for creative expressions about life, became one area in which black people could present their ideas, feelings, and needs to the American people. Furthermore, black writers made it known that there was a real need to put authentic material about blacks into the theater in place of the usual material which presented what white people thought about black life. In fact, many of the existing plays by whites contained both incorrect information and inaccurate portrayals of black life and attitudes and drew criticism from leading black writers and reviewers.

There were, however, a few plays written by whites which expressed some ideas and feelings of black people. One such play was Jean Genet's play *The Blacks,* which opened off Broadway in 1961. At this time, there was a general feeling that plays about blacks didn't have much money behind them, so had little opportunity of opening on Broadway. But *The Blacks* proved to be very successful. It had an outstanding cast, many of whom became well known in the theater world. The cast included Roscoe Lee Browne, Godfrey Cambridge, who won an Obie (an off-Broadway award) for his performance, Cicely Tyson, Charles Gordone, and Vinie Burrows.

Large numbers of whites filled the theater night after night, even though many parts of the play were considered abusive to them. Surprisingly, the whites in the audience loved the play. Some black reviewers tried to explain this strange reaction by saying that their guilt about how whites treated blacks made them sympathetic to the black plight.

That same year, *Black Bird* with dancer and actress Thelma Oliver and singer and actress Micki Grant, opened. Although the play did not have a long run on Broadway, the two actresses received good reviews and went on to other plays in which they won acclaim.

Purlie Victorious, written by the black actor and civil rights worker Ossie Davis, opened on Broadway to good reviews. The play presented hilarious scenes about efforts to establish an integrated church in a southern community, and it proved a success. Davis performed the leading role. Other cast members included his wife, Ruby Dee, and Godfrey Cambridge, Alan Alda, Sorell Booke, and Helen Martin. Several years later, the play returned to Broadway as *Purlie* with Cleavon Little and Melba Moore, who both rose to stardom in their roles.

During the 1963–1964 theater season, several black playwrights had their plays open on or off Broadway. Irving Burgie's *Ballad for Bimshire* opened in 1963 with two leading actors, Ossie Davis and Frederick O'Neal, in the cast. Burgie, who was better known for such songs as "Jamaica Farewell," "Day-O," and "I Do Adore Her," was determined to produce a play which was written by a black, produced by a black, and managed by a black. Overcoming many obstacles, the show opened on Broadway and received good black support. About

85 percent of the audiences were black. And thousands of dollars were raised for civil rights activities through theater parties.

Tambourines to Glory, Langston Hughes' play, opened in November, 1963. But the reviews were not good even though several experienced performers, including Hilda Simms, Clara Ward, and Rosetta Le Noire, were in the cast.

James Baldwin, better known for his essays and novels, had two plays open in 1963 and 1964. His first play, *The Amen Corner,* opened in Los Angeles, California. His second, *Blues for Mr. Charlie,* opened on Broadway in April of 1964 with a notable cast consisting of David Baldwin, Al Freeman, Pat Hingle, Percy Rodriguez, Diana Sands, and Rip Torn. The play was based on the deaths of a young boy, Emmett Till, and a civil rights worker, Medgar Evers, in Mississippi. There were often several outbursts of applause during parts of the play.

During the 1964–1965 season, some outstanding plays by black writers opened. LeRoi Jones' *The Toilet* and *The Slave* opened off Broadway and created a sensation among the critics. Jones was considered by some to be "the angriest young playwright" because he compared American society with the foulness of a toilet. He also called it a slave society.

Howard Da Silva and Felix Leon's *The Zulu and the Zayda* also opened during the 1965–1966 season but closed in early spring of 1966. This play explored a relationship between a Jewish grandfather and a young Zulu.

Happy Ending and *Day of Absence,* two plays by an actor named Douglas Turner Ward, illustrated the interdependence of whites and blacks.

The number of plays written by blacks grew steadily. In 1970, Charles Gordone received a Pulitzer Prize for his off-Broadway play *No Place to Be Somebody.* There was much black talent around, but Broadway was obviously not ready to accept the works of black playwrights. It became necessary to establish a means of helping these talented blacks and providing a place to perform. An actor named Robert Hooks realized the need and, eager to share his professional training with other young blacks, he started an actors' workshop in his apartment. Hooks soon included an actor named Douglas Turner Ward and a director named Gerald Krone. The three men began thinking of how they might continue to help blacks "to develop their creativity, express their unique experiences, and receive training in the theater arts." They wrote a proposal which explained their ideas and the necessary budget. Then they submitted it to the Ford Foundation, which gave them a grant of money for a three-year period. The Negro Ensemble Company was established in 1967, and a number of high-quality plays were performed. In 1968, there was *The Song of the Lusitanian Bogey*. Lonnie Elder's *Ceremonies in Dark Old Men* opened in 1969 and was a hit. It was revived on television in 1975. *The Sty of the Blind Pig* opened in 1971. And in 1972, *The River Niger* by Joseph Walker opened at the St. Marks Playhouse, then moved to Broadway in 1973 where it remained for eight months; it won the Tony Award in 1974 as the best Broadway play of the year.

Other productions were Richard Wright's *Daddy Goodness*, Derek Walcott's *The Dream on Monkey Mountain*, Paul Cartin Harrison's musical *The Great McDaddy*, and Leslie Lee's *The First Breeze of Summer*.

In an interview with Elenore Lester printed in *The New York Times* in 1975, Ward declared that the real reason for the existence of the Negro Ensemble Company is "to create the black theater that has been too long in coming in this country." But at the same time, Ward said, "The Company has fulfilled and is fulfilling the functions we had in mind when we started

The cast of the television version of Ceremonies in Dark Old Men included Rosalind Cash, Godfrey Cambridge, Douglas Turner Ward, and Robert Hooks.

to provide a center where black creative talent could be nurtured and a black audience could be built. When we started out, we got audiences that were about 80 percent white. Now the situation just about reversed itself. We also have trained 4,000 people, tuition free, in all kinds of theater work—artistic, administrative, and technical."

Also in 1967, the Urban Arts Corps was started as a pilot program financed by the New York State Council on the Arts. Over the years, numbers of black young people joined the company and moved on to success in a variety of shows. Among them are actors such as Sherman Hemsley, star of the television series "The Jeffersons" and Marvin Felix Camillo, director of the Broadway play *Short Eyes*.

Don't Bother Me I Can't Cope brought the company to the attention of many theatergoers. It opened in 1970, played in several off-Broadway theaters, and toured to six cities before having a more than two-year run on Broadway.

The original forces behind the Urban Arts Corps were Vinnette Carroll, director, and Micki Grant, an Obie Award winner and the composer-lyricist of *Don't Bother Me I Can't Cope*.

Vinnette Carroll later explained why the Urban Arts Corps was established. "We looked around then [1967] and I think what was missing was leadership for young black performers."

Musical shows provided another opportunity for blacks on Broadway. David Merrick, a white producer, revived the musical *Hello Dolly* with an all-black cast led by Pearl Bailey and Cab Calloway. Ossie Davis' *Purlie* has only two whites, necessary to play the white roles. *Raisin,* the musical version of Lorraine Hansberry's *A Raisin in the Sun,* had an all-black cast which received acclaim. In fact, the leading actress, Virginia Capers, received a Tony Award for her performance, and the play itself also received a Tony for best musical play in 1974. In addition, Broadway's first black director-choreographer, Donald McKayle, received excellent reviews. Clive Barnes, drama critic for *The New York Times* wrote:

> *The performances blaze. . . . The dance numbers rank among the best in years. Like Jerome Robbins [a leading white choreographer], Donald McKayle comes to the theater as a ranking choreographer, but also, like Mr. Robbins, his skill with actors must now be unquestioned.*

When the Negro Ensemble Theatre opened its 1974 season with Paul Carter Harrison's *The Great MacDaddy,* Clive Barnes was impressed. He reviewed the musical and wrote:

> *What we are witnessing is the birth of the black musical, with storytelling techniques and dramatic rhythms as distinct from the white musical as jazz is distinct from the Viennese waltz. . . . The Negro Ensemble Company can nowadays be relied upon for some of the best acting in town. . . . this is not your run-of-the-mill musical.*

The Black Theatre Alliance was formed in 1970 to "solve common problems, to share information and to create an instrument to validate black theater as community institutions," said Joan Sandler, executive director of the Alliance. The Alliance consisted of thirty independent black theatrical groups, many of which are based in New York. Services have been expanded to include emergency loans to member groups, theater-management training programs, quarterly letters, and fourteen theaters for touring productions.

In the late 1970s, musicals about, by, and starring blacks proved box-office successes on Broadway. *The Wiz* was a modern musical update of *The Wizard of Oz. Ain't Misbehavin'* was a musical biography of Fats Waller, and *Bubbling Brown Sugar* looked back at the days when Harlem was a swinging musical area. In New York, the Negro Ensemble Company played many dramas, and a poem-drama, *For Colored Girls Who Have Considered Suicide When the Rainbow is Enuf,* by Ntozake Shange, proved a popular Broadway success for black and white audiences alike.

CREATIVITY
THROUGH DANCE

During the mid-sixties, a number of gifted young people worked at art forms that would reflect their social and political ideas. They were dancers, film makers, playwrights, poets, and painters, all bent on creating a new black culture or on proving that blacks could excel in a variety of the creative arts.

Two dance companies which achieved both national and international fame are the Alvin Ailey American Dance Theater and the Dance Theatre of Harlem. Alvin Ailey was born in Texas and was taken to Los Angeles to live at the age of eleven. While a student at the University of California at Los Angeles, Ailey was introduced to dance at the Lester Horton Dance Theater. Ailey was fortunate in that Horton devoted much of his time to training black dancers. In 1953 Horton died, and Ailey became both artistic director and choreographer for the company. But he wanted to study modern dance and ballet in depth, so he went to New York to study with leaders in the dance field, such as Martha Graham, Doris Humphrey, Karel Shook, Charles Weidmann, and Hanya Holm. By 1958 he felt ready to lead a dance company again, and the Alvin Ailey American Dance Theater was established.

The Alvin Ailey Dance Theater is today a multiracial New York City company which tries to provide an historical presentation of dance and hopes to leave behind, as stated in the playbill of one of the company's programs, "a multiracial institution of dance repertory that preserves and transmits the essence of American dance and culture."

Clive Barnes commended Ailey in a review in the *New York Times*. "Ailey understands the theater in a way that no other choreographer understands it apart from Jerome Robbins. And this is not a compliment—merely a fact. . . . He understands jazz—he is the only choreographer who genuinely does. . . ."

An example of Ailey's desire to capture the essence of American culture is seen in his wish to preserve the variety of music which Duke Ellington composed:

Duke also liked to have his music danced. He thought that dance was a major means of communicating what he was trying to get through to people, which was a love of life and a caring about mankind. I thought . . . of all the kinds of music which he contributed over the years . . . to give to the world a portrait in dance of one of the major musical forces of the century. We had spoken about this in 1972 and had actually begun preparation when he died in 1974.

The Alvin Ailey Dance Company has developed a reputation of excellence in both dance and theater. It performs to a variety of music, including religious, blues, gospel, jazz, classical, and modern. The Company's official school, The American Dance Center, trains promising young dancers. In 1974, the Alvin Ailey Repertory Workshop was organized as part of the school to provide a means by which new audiences could be exposed to the art of dance. The workshop performs in prisons and mental health and drug rehabilitation centers, as well as for the general public and in schools throughout New York State.

Black children in ballet clothes are a familiar sight at the Dance Theatre of Harlem. The founder and driving force behind the Dance Theatre is Arthur Mitchell. He attended the High School of Performing Arts in New York City. Upon graduation, Mitchell received two scholarships, one to Bennington College in Vermont and one to the School of American Ballet, the New

York City Ballet's official school. Mitchell decided to attend the School of American Ballet.

After three years, Mitchell felt that there was little chance for a black man to achieve success as a classical dancer in the United States. Traditionally, blacks had to achieve fame in Europe before gaining recognition in the United States. So Mitchell left for Europe. While there, he received a wire from the New York City Ballet asking him to join the company.

In November, 1955, Mitchell made his debut with the New York City Ballet, dancing in George Balanchine's "Western Symphony." He performed in numerous other roles, having his greatest early success in 1957 in the title role of "Agon," one of several roles which Balanchine created for him. For about two decades, Mitchell danced with the New York City Ballet, and he became the first black principal dancer in ballet during the 1960s.

In 1968, Mitchell was deeply moved by the assassination of Dr. Martin Luther King, Jr. He reacted to this tragic loss by becoming determined to work with other blacks within the field that he knew best—dance. He decided to teach ballet to black children.

In 1968, Mitchell asked Karel Shook, ballet master of the Netherlands Ballet, to work with him to establish ballet classes in Harlem. Two years later, the newly established Dance Theatre of Harlem became the first permanently established black ballet company in the United States. The company went on to perform throughout the nation and in several European countries.

MUSIC:
NEW EXPERIENCES

Through the fifties, sixties and early seventies, black musicians continued to participate in many different types of musical experiences. Some maintained or brought changes to traditional black music. Others created musical compositions or performed in areas such as opera, choral, and symphonic music which had not been previously open to black musicians.

The traditional black music called *old country blues* was increasingly replaced by loud big-city blues. Electric guitars and saxophones pushed the new big-city blues toward more noise, more excitement, and a strong beat. By the early fifties, a new style emerged. It became known as rhythm and blues. Small bands of five or six pieces belted out this new-style black music under the leadership of musicians such as Louis Jordan and Fats Domino.

In 1951, a white disk jockey named Alan Freed started a series of "rhythm reviews" in Cleveland which drew huge crowds. Black musicians continued to play rhythm and blues for mostly white audiences, but the music was banned by white radio stations. Freed decided that to avoid further banning of the music associated with blacks, he would drop the term *rhythm and blues* and use *rock and roll* instead.

Then rock and roll changed. Elvis Presley, the white rock singer, came from a southern background in which he was exposed to rhythm and blues, fundamental revival singing, and country ballads. Presley's singing was a mixture of all three, and he became a hit with teenagers.

Fats Domino, however, continued to play rhythm and blues, and by 1960, he had sold about fifty million records. Other

Diana Ross and The Supremes, delivering the Motown Sound in 1968.

blacks, such as Diana Ross and The Supremes, started their careers as rhythm-and-blues singers. Ray Charles was considered one of the best of the early group, along with James Brown, who could work an audience up into a frenzy.

Soon there was a new dance craze among the young and the old—the Twist—which really wasn't new at all. The original song about the Twist was written in 1958 by Hank Ballard and became a hit in 1961. The peppermint Lounge off Times Square in New York City became "the" place to go to dance the Twist. Chubby Checker cut the hit record "Let's Twist Again" which swept the country and had young children, teenagers, and adults doing the Twist.

The Twist, however, didn't last long. Soon young people were doing many new dances. There was the Fly, the Pong, the Popeye, the Mashed Potato, the Dog, the Monkey, the Waddle, the Frug, the Jerk, the Boogaloo, and the Funky Broadway among many others.

Another form of popular music, called *soul,* came into being. Soul could be described as updated rhythm and blues. This new music had the rhythm style and a great deal of gospel. The beat of rhythm and blues remained, but the music became more passionate and heated. That was soul.

James Brown was a leading soul singer. His background in a southern gospel quartet made it easy for Brown to sing the new music called soul.

Ray Charles, a blind singer, is given credit for taking soul to different parts of the world. He sang about experiences and emotions to which everyone could relate and thereby communicated with the listener. The Ray Charles sound was made up of his band, his voice, his piano, and a total extension of himself to the listener. For these reasons, Ray Charles had been called a genius. His style is that of a classical blues singer. Charles'

Ray Charles combined rhythm and blues with spiritual, or gospel music, to produce one of the most popular forms of music in the sixties, called soul.

call-and-response singing with a chorus and his unique piano style and sound all blend together to make him different from the usual popular musician. According to Charles, "in jazz, when you get rid of the melody, you put yourself in." However, within his works, several aspects of blues can be found. There are touches of the spiritual, the gospel chorus, the work song, and the folk song. In fact, it has been said that Charles' musical history is black history.

Aretha Franklin's success as a contemporary singer is based on her gospel background. Her mother sang gospel music. And at the age of ten, Aretha was a part of her father's (the Reverend C. L. Franklin) traveling troupe of evangelists. By the time she was eighteen, Aretha Franklin wanted to make it on her own. Thus, Aretha Franklin started on her way to career and success. Today she is considered one of the leading gospel singers.

The master of blues guitar is B. B. King. As a boy, B. B. sang in church choirs and started playing the guitar. Born on a Mississippi Delta cotton plantation near Indianola, Mississippi, in 1925, he dropped out of high school when the money he could make working in the fields became important to his survival.

In 1947, B. B. went north to Memphis and lived with a cousin, Bukka White, who played slide guitar. There, he developed a style of his own. B. B. was first billed as Riley King (his real name), the "Blues Boy from Beale Street" in Memphis. The billing was later shortened to the "Beale Street Blues Boy" and finally to just "B. B." In 1949, B. B. started recording, and after several releases, "Three O'Clock Blues" was a hit. This success encouraged B. B. to begin touring and gathering a following which continues to grow.

The black singer named Stevie Wonder has been blind

since his birth in 1951. However, this handicap did not discourage Stevie Wonder from achieving a career in music which has so far won him five Grammy awards.

Other popular black musicians, such as Ella Fitzgerald, continue to excite audiences and to maintain their fame. In 1974, the University of Maryland dedicated the Ella Fitzgerald School of Performing Arts, a $1.6 million building, the first such structure in the nation to be named for a black artist.

Big bands, which were once the rage in dance halls and movie theaters, soon became too expensive to maintain. By the 1970s most of the big bands were replaced by small combos of three, four, or five players. However, a few of the more popular big bands survived.

Count Basie still attracts large audiences. Duke Ellington, like Basie, also led his big band in performances before numerous enthusiastic audiences. In 1971, Ellington was elected to the Songwriters' Hall of Fame at the organization's first annual awards dinner. He died in 1974, leaving more than six thousand compositions, ranging from popular tunes to complex classical and sacred music.

One gospel singer was mourned by thousands when she died. Mahalia Jackson, who died in 1972, was remembered not only for her gospel singing but also for her participation in the civil rights movement. She gave much of her own money to the movement and sang special concerts to raise additional funds.

As more opportunities became available in the popular music field, more blacks achieved fame. Some of those who continue to draw large crowds to their performances are Sammy Davis, Jr., Dizzy Gillespie, Lionel Hampton, Oscar Peterson, and Sarah Vaughan. Several younger performers, such as Diana Ross, Dionne Warwick, and Roberta Flack, are holding their places in the long list of popular musical performers.

In classical music, many new personalities gained recognition from the early 1960s on. A major breakthrough into the white world of opera was achieved by a soprano named Leontyne Price. She was born in Laurel, Mississippi, in 1927. After graduating from college in Ohio, Ms. Price won a scholarship to Julliard School of Music. During the 1950s she appeared on Broadway for a short time in *Four Saints In Three Acts* before going on tour with *Porgy and Bess*. She appeared and performed in several operas for the NBC-TV Opera Company before making her 1961 debut in *Il Trovatore* at the Metropolitan Opera House in New York City. In 1966, Ms. Price achieved high acclaim and honor when she was chosen to open the Metropolitan Opera season in *Anthony and Cleopatra*.

Between her debut in 1961 and 1969 she gave 118 performances at the Metropolitan Opera House. Ms. Price has thought about her success and her struggles as a black singer in a white-dominated field and has remarked:

> *As a token black, I paid my dues. I realize that because I am black, I will still always be on kind of a duty. There are still many things that have to be done. It is kind of wonderful, though, that they're divided in half. . . . To be able to concentrate on being a plain singer, without the overwhelming weight . . . on your back. . . . I think it has been lightened, not completely pulled together, but lightened.*

An understanding of the difficulties that black singers faced as well as a desire to provide opportunities for blacks to sing opera stimulated the establishment of a company known as Opera/South. In 1971, three colleges in the Jackson, Mississippi, area supported the establishment of Opera/South. The colleges were

Jackson State University, Tougaloo College, and Utica Junior College. Students from the colleges sang in the chorus, built sets, and designed costumes. The purpose of Opera/South was to give students a chance to work in professional surroundings, to showcase young black professionals ready to sing leading roles, to perform the works of new American composers, and to bring opera to new audiences. By the mid-seventies, Opera/South had accomplished all its objectives.

In 1968, Henry Lewis became the first black music director of a leading American orchestra when the New Jersey Symphony appointed him to that post. A second success for Lewis occurred in 1972, when the Metropolitan Opera engaged him, as the first black conductor in the history of the company, to conduct *La Bohème*. Previously, Lewis had conducted the San Francisco Opera, the Vancouver Opera, the Boston Opera, and the American Opera Society, as well as major symphony orchestras. However, in the field of symphonic music, the overall number of blacks remains quite small.

Because blacks have traditionally kept out of symphony orchestras, many classical musicians go to Europe to study and to seek employment. Some efforts are being made to correct the situation. The Commission on Human Rights has pressured such organizations as the New York Philharmonic and the Metropolitan Opera to make an effort to hire people from minority groups. Some orchestras, such as the Los Angeles Philharmonic, have programs which provide instruction in symphonic music for minority-group musicians.

In 1965, the Symphony of the New World was founded by a white conductor, the late Benjamin Steinberg, together with several black and white musicians. The organization used black conductors and soloists and played the music of black composers. Although the orchestra was integrated, its prime purpose was to give minority-group musicians opportunities to play symphonic music.

Another organization which was organized specifically to help blacks is the Afro-American Music Opportunities Association (AAMOA), which is located in Minneapolis. AAMOA maintains a list of players eligible for orchestra jobs. The staff works with Columbia Records to see that albums devoted to music by black composers are released. They help to sponsor events such as the Black Composers' Symposium which was held by the Houston Symphony.

In New York, four young musicians, Carman Moore, Leonard Groins, and Kermit and Dorothy De Costa, founded the Society of Black Composers in 1968. The membership was made up of about thirty black composers and thirty-five other musicians, and many of them had classical music training. The purpose of the organization was to perform the works of young black composers, and an ensemble was maintained to do so through a yearly series of concerts.

Some of the new compositions performed by the ensemble combined black traditional music and jazz with modern classical music. One of the founders, Carman Moore, has already gained recognition for his work. In 1974, the New York Philharmonic commissioned Moore to compose a composition entitled *Wildfires and Field Song,* which was conducted by Pierre Boulez. Moore uses combinations of voices and instruments that tend to be unusual. For example, two movements of *Gospel Fuse* have parts for an orchestra, a female vocal quartet, a pianist, an organist, a soprano saxophone, and contain both classical and jazz music. For a performance in Hong Kong, Moore brought together Chinese instruments, a jazz quintet, and a symphony orchestra. This kind of new combinations is bringing a new sound to the classical musical stage. In 1976, Moore's home city of Elyria, Ohio, commissioned him to write a cantata entitled *The Great American Nebula,* which will have a narrator and a text about outer space. Carman Moore has truly made great strides in bringing new musical combinations to the concert stage.

On the concert stage, a young black pianist by the name of Andre Watts earned wide acclaim. In 1962, Andre was a sixteen-year-old unknown pianist from Philadelphia. By 1963, Watts had become the first classical musical artist to have his solo recital televised live from Lincoln Center in New York City. Young Watts was performing in a New York Philharmonic Young People's Concert conducted by Leonard Bernstein at the time.

There is still a significant group of black children today who hope to continue their studies in classical music. Some of these students are found in high school orchestras and choruses around the country.

One such group of students in New York City is in the All-City Concert Choir. The choir is made up of former and present members of the All-City High School Chorus. These young people perform for visiting state, national, and international dignitaries. They also perform at leading music centers such as Lincoln Center.

PROTEST THROUGH LITERATURE

Beginning in the 1950s, creative young blacks protested black life in America through literature. Many of their writings gained attention throughout the nation, and some even received international acclaim. Black bookstores such as Harlem's National Memorial African Bookstore, and Ellis in Chicago contained numerous publications of young black authors. Some of the works were printed by large white publishing companies, while others were published by small black companies. Some anthologies were mimeographed by the writers themselves.

For many of the young writers, poetry seemed to be the preferred medium for expressing their observations, interpretations, and anger about black life in America. However, some wrote novels, and others produced plays. During the 1960s, many of the newly created works reflected the three major themes of the civil rights revolution—liberation, self-determination, and a positive identity.

Gwendolyn Brooks, born in Topeka, Kansas, in 1917, is poet-laureate of the state of Illinois and a winner of several awards, including the Pulitzer Prize for poetry in 1950 for her poems in *Annie Allen*. She was further honored by being made a Fellow of the American Academy of Arts and Letters, an organization of admired and successful writers. Another high honor was given to Ms. Brooks in 1973 when she was named to a three-year term as an honorary consultant in American letters to the Library of Congress.

Ms. Brooks has published several books of poetry which describe life in the black ghetto. Her first book of poetry is entitled *A Street in Bronzeville* and is found in the libraries of schools around the country. Her early work reflected her relief that her feelings about herself were conditioned by the white world. However, her later works, such as *Riot* published in 1969, revealed a change to the liberation poetry of the sixties.

The Invisible Man, Ralph Ellison's only novel, was published in 1952. Almost immediately, Ellison became a celebrity, and was considered among the top American writers. The novel received the National Book Award in 1952, and in 1964, it was named by two hundred writers and critics as the most distinguished single work of the previous twenty years. In the novel, Ellison uses black folk culture to develop the theme of a search for identity and to illustrate that whites did not really see or understand blacks. Ellison wrote:

> *All my life I had been looking for something, and everywhere I turned someone tried to tell me what it was. I accepted their answers too, though they were often in contradiction. . . . I was looking for myself and asking everyone except myself questions which I, and only I, could answer. . . . I had to discover that I am an invisible man!*

Ellison was born in Oklahoma in 1914. In 1976, he became a board member of the American Academy and Institute of Arts and Letters.

Another writer widely quoted during the 1960s was James Baldwin. Born in 1924 in Harlem, he showed skill in writing while still in high school. In fact, he was editor of his school magazine. Three years after graduation, Baldwin won a Eugene Saxton Fellowship to further his studies.

Baldwin's nonfiction analyzed the prejudices and hatred of whites toward blacks, and morality among whites. One reviewer called Baldwin's works "stinging, insulting to white readers, and

[it] carries an undisguised challenge not only as to the quality of the morality, but to their mentality as well." Some of Baldwin's novels are *Go Tell It on the Mountain, Giovanni's Room,* and *Another Country.* Two collections of essays, *Nobody Knows My Name* and *Notes of a Native Son,* helped to establish Baldwin as a major American writer. *The Fire Next Time,* another novel, supported Baldwin's earlier successes by being an immediate best seller.

Baldwin also turned to the theater and wrote two plays, *Blues for Mr. Charlie* and *The Amen Corner* which were produced on Broadway. Baldwin's many essays, articles, novels, and short stories describe the experiences and views of urban black America and protest against both negative white attitudes and poor treatment of black people.

Imamu Baraka was born Le Roi Jones in 1934 in Newark, New Jersey. He published his first book, *Preface to a Twenty Volume Suicide Note,* in 1961, and won a John Hay Whitney Fellowship in the same year for his poetry and fiction. He produced several books, such as *Blues People* (1963), *The Dead Lecturer* (1964), and *The System of Dante's Hell* (1965).

During the early 1960s, Baraka also wrote several plays which used racial conflict as a major theme. His play *The Dutchman* (1964) received the Obie award for the best off-Broadway show of that year. *The Slave* and *The Toilet* (both 1965) were stinging evaluations of American society. Baraka was also recognized for his numerous articles on jazz and jazz musicians. During the 1970s, he became active in civil rights projects.

Soul on Ice, a book of sharp commentary on American racism, was written by Eldridge Cleaver in 1968 while in Soledad Prison in California. It soon became a best-seller. Cleaver was born in 1935 in Wabhaseka, Arkansas. By the time he was in his early twenties, he had served several prison terms, but at the age of twenty-two, he decided to change his ways and develop his writing ability. He began reading and writing essays in which he criticized the American way of life. He became the minister of information of the Black Panther Party and later worked for *Ramparts* magazine. His membership in the Black Panther organization brought him into the midst of a shoot-out with the Oakland, California, police. A legal battle won Cleaver freedom long enough for him to run for president of the United States on the Peace and Freedom party ticket. He gave speeches and wrote articles about what he thought was wrong with American society. He often suggested cures which were considered revolutionary by some people.

Don L. Lee is a young black poet whose work has both a political and humanitarian function. In his book *Think Black* (1968), Lee states, "Black art will elevate and enlighten our people and lead them toward an awareness of self, i.e., their blackness. It will show them mirrors, beautiful symbols, and will aid in the destruction of anything nasty and detrimental to our advancement as a people."

One of the most popular young black writers of the sixties was Nikki Giovanni. She was born in Knoxville, Tennessee, in 1943, but she grew up in Cincinnati, Ohio. At Fisk University, Ms. Giovanni joined the Writers' Workshop and helped to establish a chapter of the Student Nonviolent Coordinating Committee. She returned to Cincinnati before graduating and worked in black cultural programs. In some of her poetry, she makes angry demands for action on the part of black people.

By the 1970s, there were fewer black protest publications. Some of the poets continued to produce such literature, but the emphasis in black literature began to change.

One black writer looked and traveled to Africa in search

of his roots. Alex Haley, coauthor of *The Autobiography of Malcolm X,* worked for twelve years to gather information about his ancestors. This work took him all the way back to Gambia, in Africa. His search for a particular black ancestor named Kunta Kinte became an important link between African and American history. When Haley felt that he had achieved his purpose, he used his newfound information to write the novel *Roots*. Published in 1976, it was soon a record-breaking bestseller.

1980:
ASSESSING THE ISSUES
AND PROBLEMS

The new decade began with the twentieth anniversary celebration of the first lunch counter sit-in. On February 1, 1980, four black men, Joseph McNeil, Franklin McCain, David Richmond, and Ezell Blair, Jr. (who has changed his name to Jibreel Khazan) went to the same lunch counter at the F. W. Woolworth store in Greensboro, North Carolina, where four black students (McNeil and McCain among them) were refused service twenty years ago. The purpose of this return visit was to call attention to the original sit-in that launched a new thrust within the civil rights movement.

Officials of both the city of Greensboro and the F. W. Woolworth store celebrated the occasion with the four men while other citizens prepared themselves for an anti-Ku Klux Klan march and rally that was to take place the next day. The planned march was a vivid reminder that groups such as the Ku Klux Klan were still functioning in spite of the gains made in the civil rights movement. In fact, such hate groups were existing openly in the North and the West as well as the South.

Blacks in positions to be heard spoke out about the issues and problems that continued to plague black communities. The black Commissioner of Employment in New York City, Ronald T. Gault, reported that the jobs that were becoming available required education and training. Horace W. Morris, director of the New York Urban League, expressed his opinion about black unemployment, suggesting that public education was the key to the remedy. He said, "The only way to attract new jobs to the city is for the city to offer a skilled labor force to fill these jobs . . . More money to the schools is not the answer. There needs to be a generation of will and leadership by public officials and the private sector to attack the problem."

The unemployment problem among blacks was nationwide. During 1979, black unemployment nationally was 11.3 percent while the total for the nation was 5.8 percent.

In Chicago, members of black organizations focused on another problem. They believed that Chicago was more racially biased in the 1970s than was the South in the 1950s. The organizations representing a variety of groups such as the Chicago Urban League, People United to Save Humanity (PUSH), Cook County Bar Association, and individuals in the city council, state legislature, as well as ministers, formed a coalition to do the following:

1. Make appeals for equality in corporate boardrooms.
2. File civil rights lawsuits.
3. Boycott certain downtown businesses.
4. Tie up city council legislation deemed harmful.
5. Seek increased political power including a major push to elect the city's first black mayor in 1982.

Bernice Johnson Reagon, director of the program in Black American Culture at the Smithsonian Institution in Washington, D.C., held a conference, entitled "Voices of the Civil Rights Movement," to recall the work of the movement and plan ahead for the future. Many of the conference participants were the students and organizers of civil rights activities during the 1960s. Presently, they hold a variety of different jobs such as teachers, elected officials, songwriters, community developers, and stockbrokers.

Some of them wondered if their past work in the movement had really improved America. "Everything has changed and nothing has changed," said the Reverend Dr. Wyatt Tee Walker, a former leading personality in the Southern Christian Leadership Conference during the 1960s. He continued, "The condition of the black man in America has not changed substantially since 1619."

John Lewis, once chairman of the Student Nonviolent Coordinating Committee (SNCC), said, "I see another nonviolent wave using some of the same techniques and tactics of the 1960s. We must continue to build the idea of a beloved community where one sees people as human beings."

Another conference participant, who was the first chairman of SNCC and is presently mayor of Washington, D.C., Marion Barry, spoke of the civil rights movement of the 1960s as a beginning. He said,

> *The struggle has just begun in the sense that we did something to change the face of America, we did something to change the lives of some people, but not nearly enough to change the lives of enough people. . . . We have to stand up and fight, we have to stand up and struggle, we have to stand up and make sacrifices. But, more important, we have to stand up.*

Thus the new decade began with blacks still keenly aware of the ever present need to continue the civil rights movement into the 1980s.

FOR FURTHER READING

Abdul, Raoul. *Famous Black Entertainers of Today.* New York: Dodd, Mead, 1974.

Adoff, Arnold, ed. *Celebrations: A New Anthology of Black American Poetry.* Chicago: Follett Publishing, 1977.

Fax, Elton C. *Contemporary Black Leaders.* New York: Dodd, Mead, 1970.

Fine, Elsa Honig, *The Afro-American Artist: A Search for Identity.* New York: Holt, Rinehart & Winston, Inc., 1973.

Haskins, James. *The Life and Death of Martin Luther King, Jr.* New York: Lothrop, Lee & Shepard, 1977.

Thum, Marcella. *Exploring Black America: A History and Guide.* New York: Atheneum, 1975.

INDEX

ABOUT THE AUTHOR

Dr. Florence Jackson is presently Director of Social Studies, New York City School District, having held positions as a teacher, supervisor, and administrator in the city schools. She has worked for other organizations and agencies such as The Center for Urban Education, and National Assessment of Educational Progress.

As a consultant to publishers, regional and city educational television, state education departments, and universities, Dr. Jackson has broadened her knowledge and experience in social studies education. She has served on the board of directors of the National Council for the Social Studies, as well as similar organizations.

Dr. Jackson received a scholarship to study at the University of Nairobi, Kenya, and has a Doctorate in Urban Education from Fordham University. Her other awards include Women of Achievement, Leadership in Bicentennial Programs, and Achievement in Cultural Leadership.